Coping™

COPING WITH
BREAKUPS
AND JEALOUSY

Tamra B. Orr

Rosen
YA™
New York

For Rebekah

Published in 2018 by The Rosen Publishing Group, Inc.
29 East 21st Street, New York, NY 10010

Copyright © 2018 by The Rosen Publishing Group, Inc.

First Edition

Library of Congress Cataloging-in-Publication Data

Names: Orr, Tamra B., author.
Title: Coping with breakups and jealousy / Tamra B. Orr.
Description: First edition. | New York, NY : Rosen Publishing, 2018. | Series: Coping |
Audience: Grades 7–12. | Includes bibliographical references and index.
Identifiers: ISBN 9781508173885 (library bound)
Subjects: LCSH: Dating (Social customs)—Juvenile literature. | Love—Juvenile literature. | Separation (Psychology)—Juvenile literature. | Jealousy—Juvenile literature. | Interpersonal relations—Juvenile literature.
Classification: LCC HQ801.O77 2018 | DDC 306.73—dc23

Manufactured in the United States of America

CONTENTS

Introduction 4

CHAPTER ONE
The Green-Eyed Monster 7

CHAPTER TWO
Building Trust in Yourself and Others 22

CHAPTER THREE
Breaking Up Is Hard to Do 43

CHAPTER FOUR
Getting Back Up After the Fall 67

CHAPTER FIVE
Life Lessons Learned 86

GLOSSARY 99
FOR MORE INFORMATION 101
FOR FURTHER READING 104
BIBLIOGRAPHY 106
INDEX 109

INTRODUCTION

Jonas pulled his phone out of his pocket and sent yet another text to Katie. He checked Facebook and Instagram one more time to see if she had posted any more photos of her and her new coworker, Brandon. No new pictures—yet. Just the one she had posted yesterday from the store's employee appreciation party. Jonas could feel his heart beating quickly. He was sweating and felt tense from his head to his feet. He pictured Katie laughing and flirting with Brandon while she was at work. She was probably too busy paying attention to him to answer Jonas's texts.

Sighing, Jonas flopped down on his bed. He had been dating Katie for three months now, and he thought they were doing great—until Brandon came along. Katie got along really well with him and always came over after work with another story of what the two of them had done at the store. Maybe we should just break up, Jonas thought. He imagined how he would do it. Maybe he could text her when she got off of work? He winced.

No, texting seemed like a pretty cold way of ending a relationship. He should do it face to face. Would Katie cry or be relieved? Would he yell at her? How would they handle seeing each other in school after that? It would feel really awkward, wouldn't it?

It is easy to feel jealous when a new person enters the picture. However, it is extremely important to determine if your partner is just being friendly or flirting.

Jonas did not want to break up. He really enjoyed being with Katie, but he hated feeling so jealous. What should he do about it?

You may have felt like Jonas before or even like Katie. Relationships are a normal part of life, but, unfortunately, so is trouble within them. One of the biggest issues you may face is feeling jealous. A little spark of jealousy can be all right. It means the relationship is important to you and you want to protect it. However, just as a little may serve to regulate boundaries in a relationship, more is often negative, and even destructive. Jealousy can ruin a relationship and can make life miserable for everyone. It can also lead to a breakup, another painful experience.

While it is almost inevitable that the majority of romantic relationships you have as a teen will run into trouble and eventually end, how you respond to these conflicts and breakups is under your control. This book will help you understand how jealousy impacts a relationship and how to cope with it, including how to know when the emotion has crossed a line into abuse. It will also explore how to survive a breakup, whether you happen to be on the sending or receiving end. Finally, this book will show you how to recover from the end of a relationship and find ways to learn from it and move on to bigger and better connections in the future.

CHAPTER ONE

The Green-Eyed Monster

Being in love feels wonderful, but being jealous tends to feel miserable. Often, however, one leads right to the other. Jealousy has many different definitions, including "disposed to suspect rivalry or unfaithfulness" or, as psychiatrist and professor at Weill Cornell University Medical School Dr. Robert Leahy called it in an article for *Psychology Today*, "angry, agitated worry."

Jealousy is considered a natural emotion that may pop up in your friendships, in family dynamics, with coworkers, and certainly in romantic relationships. "Jealousy is a universal emotion," continues Leahy. "Evolutionary psychologist David Buss in *The Dangerous Passion* makes a good case that jealousy has evolved as a mechanism to defend our interests. After all, our ancestors who drove off competitors were more likely to have their genes survive . . . Jealousy was a way in which vital interests could be defended."

Jealousy not only makes you feel uncomfortable, but it can also make you doubt yourself and damage your self-esteem. It can even spoil special occasions and events.

One teen, Vanessa van Petten, wrote about jealousy on her blog, giving advice to parents who struggled with teens experiencing the emotion. "Remind them (teens) that jealousy is completely normal and that essentially everybody has experienced it," she wrote. "Although this one might seem quite obvious, sometimes it is easy for teens to forget and for them to just simply believe that they are feeling this way because they aren't 'good enough.'"

Jealousy can even occur in open relationships, those where each partner has agreed to date other people, while maintaining their personal connection. On the teen site "Yo Expert," the idea of open relationships is explored, and one of the members wrote, "If you occasionally feel a little jealous, that's to be expected, no matter how open or closed the relationship. However if

Why Green?

Sadness is blue. Anger is red. Jealousy is green—but why? According to some theories, jealousy started being associated with the color green thanks to a number of works of classic literature. There is a reference in William Shakespeare's play *Othello*. The main character in this tragedy, Othello, is tricked (by the person he believes to be his best friend, Iago) into thinking his wife, Desdemona, has betrayed him by being unfaithful. The conniving Iago further manipulates Othello by pretending to warn him about the dangers of jealousy in Act 3, Scene 3:

> "O, beware, my lord, of jealousy;
> It is the green-eyed monster which doth mock
> The meat it feeds on; that cuckold who lives in bliss
> Who, certain of this fate, loves not his wronger;
> But, O, what damned minutes tells he o'er
> Who dotes, yet doubts, suspects, yet strongly loves!"

But it wasn't just Shakespeare who associated the color green with jealousy. Authors Ovid and Geoffrey Chaucer referred to people being "green with envy." Other experts give the credit to the ancient Greeks, who believed that a jealous person tended to produce too much bile, and, in turn, that turned the person's skin a nasty shade of green.

you feel a strong, bitter jealous feeling whenever your partner talks to someone attractive, or when they do something without you, then an open relationship may not be healthy for you."

The Same or Different?

Is jealousy the same thing as envy? The two might come up together in a thesaurus, but they are quite different. When you envy something, it means you covet or desire it—it could be your best friend's curly hair, your brother's test scores, a teacher's new sports car, or a celebrity's huge net worth. Envy means you wish you had what someone else has. Jealousy, on the other hand, means you are afraid you are going to be replaced or that you will lose someone you care about to another person.

How Jealousy Creeps In

Just how does jealousy creep into a relationship? The root of this emotion is simple: a deep fear of loss. It is often the fear of losing a person and your relationship with him or her, but it can be more than that. It can also be the fear of losing self-respect, of people or peers pitying you or seeing you negatively, or losing face in the social world.

Jealousy is an emotion that is largely born out of insecurity. Lack of self-confidence can come from many

Jealousy can end up taking much of your time and mental energy. You may find that checking up on a partner soon becomes an obsessive behavior.

directions and is often a mixture of several factors. It might be due to ongoing criticism from your family or friends. It might come from an academic struggle or a chronic health condition. Those feelings of self-doubt often result in constant comparison. If you feel like others are smarter, prettier, stronger, thinner, or (insert your choice of word here!) than you, it is easy to imagine your partner gravitating to that person. This is where jealousy comes in.

Often your feelings of inadequacy come from inside your own mind! According to many psychologists, most people have what has been termed a "critical inner voice." This is not your conscience—it does not tell you what is right or wrong or have anything to do with your morals or values. Instead, it is the voice that seems to talk to you when you look in the mirror, glance through a beauty magazine, or watch professional athletes and celebrities on television.

Dr. Lisa Firestone, author of *Conquer Your Critical Voice*, tells the online publication *Psych Alive*:

> *In order to challenge our insecurity, we have to first get to know our critical inner voice. We should try to catch it each and every time is creeps into our minds . . . Sometimes, it may be easy. We're getting dressed to go out on a date, and it screeches, "You look awful! You're so fat. Just cover yourself up. He'll never*

Jealousy can often arise in group settings when a person interprets a partner's innocent interactions, or the reactions of other friends, as inappropriate flirting.

be attracted to you." Other times, it'll be more sneaky, even soothing sounding, "Just keep to yourself. Don't invest or show her how you feel, and you won't get hurt." Identifying this critical inner voice is the first step to challenging it.

A critical inner voice eats at your self-confidence. It works to convince you that everyone else is better than you, so of course your partner is going to eventually figure that out and move on to someone better. It is the negative thoughts, beliefs, and attitudes people have that work against their own best interests. They turn a person into his or her own worst enemy, and such insecurity is a frequent cause of jealousy and jealous behaviors.

Jealousy in LGBTQ Relationships

For LGBTQ couples, jealousy can present some unusual issues. For example, what happens when one of the people involved in a lesbian relationship feels like hanging out with some of her female friends? How do you handle it if your partner wants some "girl time" that doesn't involve you? As Frankie Bashan writes on the website Your Tango, "Many women struggle with ways to walk the tightrope when telling their partner that they want time with the 'girls' —but not their girlfriend." Also, what happens in a relationship between two men if one of you wants to spend time with the guys—but not with your partner?

This kind of situation can get complicated quickly if you don't take the time to talk it out and explain your feelings to your partner. Admit you are feeling jealous, and pinpoint the cause of it—the way he or she looks at the new person in math class, the way he or she smiles when talking about the lab partner, etc. Are your jealous feelings valid, or do you just have an overactive imagination? Same-sex couples often have enough complications to deal with in today's society, so work hard not to make jealousy another hurdle to overcome.

Scientific studies seem to support these ideas. In the *Journal of Development Psychology*, experts discovered that adolescents with low self-esteem tend to worry a great deal that their relationships (both with friends and partners) will be threatened by others. Unfortunately, jealousy does more than make a person feel inadequate. It can ripple effect into depression, anger, and even aggressive behavior. It certainly can damage, or even end, relationships.

For guys, jealousy tends to manifest in anger and frustration, sometimes leading to violence. In girls, it tends to show up as sadness and depression. As Dr. Dion Metzger, author and psychiatrist, tells this author, "Any kind of flirting with the opposite sex or around a young person can cause a bad feeling in the pit of the stomach. Teens tend to not always feel comfortable in their own skin. Every gender is insecure about different things." She also says, "Girls tend to start comparing themselves, 'she has longer hair or bigger breasts so he likes her better.' With boys, they tend to compare height or athleticism." Girls tend to be perceived as more susceptible to jealousy than guys. One possible reason, though far from a definitive answer as to why, is that girls may have higher standards when it comes to commitment, kindness, empathy, and loyalty.

Feelings of jealousy, if left bottled up or ignored in a relationship, can build up over time and eventually result in hostility and conflict, including arguments.

Heed the Signs

Jealousy feels lousy, and it can often be toxic to relationships. Are you a jealous person? Check out the following list of telltale signs of jealousy. Do you see yourself reflected in the list of behaviors and signs? How about your partner? How about those you hope to date or have dated in the past? Do you or your partner:

- Question what the other is doing and need details in order to believe what you are hearing is the truth?
- Indirectly, directly, or passive-aggressively accuse the other of flirting or cheating?
- Request that your partner not socialize with anyone of the opposite gender (or same if a same-sex couple)?
- Check Facebook, Instagram, or other social media sites obsessively for any updates from your partner?
- Spy on the other's calls, emails, and text messages?
- Criticize the other for flirting or other types of behavior (real or imagined)?
- Act cold or indifferent to your partner if he or she talks to someone attractive?
- Find yourself either feeling controlled or wanting

Jealous feelings can lead to physical confrontations. A jealous boyfriend might end up fighting someone he perceives as threatening his relationship.

to control your partner's social activities?

- Obsess about what the other one is doing and if he or she is lying to you?
- Picture the other finding someone else whenever he or she is not with you?
- Experience anger or depression within the relationship?

Clearly, jealousy is hurtful to you and to your partner. It can easily become the lethal blow that puts an end to your relationship. It stems from feelings of insecurity and the fear of losing someone that is important to you. A good relationship can take a great deal of work, and jealousy only adds more stress on top of other ones. Can this green-eyed monster be tamed before it destroys everything in its path? The answer to that question is "Absolutely."

CHAPTER TWO

Building Trust in Yourself and Others

Kendra looked across the room and saw Sarah chatting with the cute red-headed barista again. Did Sarah come here for the coffee or the service, Kendra wondered. She could feel herself getting upset, just imagining that the barista and Sarah were—right this minute—exchanging cell numbers. Tears sprang to her eyes. Just then Sarah looked over at her, smiled, and blew her a kiss. Kendra took a deep breath and sat up straighter. She was letting her imagination run away with her—and lead her straight into jealousy. She smiled back at Sarah and forced herself to relax.

Jealousy may be a normal response to seeing your special someone talking with an attractive person, but how you respond to those feelings

Some instances of jealousy might be partially justified based on someone's behavior. Take the opportunity to challenge that person on the perhaps questionable judgment used.

is completely up to you. In Kendra's case, she took a moment to realize that she was picturing behavior that she did not really know was happening, and she was fortunately able to let those negative feelings go. What can you do to combat the jealous feelings you have about your partner—or the ones your partner clearly has about you?

Close Your Eyes—Working Through Jealous Feelings

Working to get over your tendency to be jealous can be difficult. Here is one way to focus on finding better, calmer ways to respond.

First, find a comfortable place to sit. (You can also do this lying down, but don't get so comfortable you risk falling asleep!) Make sure you will have a little time to be alone. Turn off your phone so no one can interrupt with a call or a text.

Next, close your eyes. Take a few deep, slow breaths. Feel yourself start to relax. Starting at your feet, imagine each part of your body relaxing. Imagine the muscles just letting go. Work your way up from your feet, to your legs, torso, arms, neck, and head.

Now, when you are ready, imagine a situation in which you might feel jealous. It might be a picture of your partner hanging out with someone else, talking and laughing. It could be an image of your partner flirting with someone at work or school. Imagine yourself seeing the situation but remaining calm and even somewhat disinterested in what is happening. Visualize that person behaving in ways that typically make you feel jealous, and then imagine yourself not responding with jealousy, but instead, with a calm and relaxed manner. The more you can visualize such a reaction, the easier it will become to transfer it to your everyday experience and for you to draw upon it when you feel jealousy in real life.

First of all, admit what you are feeling. Acknowledge the emotion. Accept it and allow it. "You don't have to 'get rid of the feeling,'" Dr. Leahy writes in *Psychology Today*. "We have found that mindfully standing back and observing that a feeling is there can often lead to the feeling weakening on its own."

Calm Down and Let Go

Dealing with feelings of jealousy is a great deal like dealing with feelings of anger, as the two emotions are closely related. If the feelings are strong enough, it can even interfere with your ability to appreciate your relationship. "Some adolescents end up worrying so much about their relationships, they don't get to enjoy them because they are always protecting them . . . and become preoccupied with whether they will last," says Jeffrey G. Parker, PhD, associate psychology professor at Pennsylvania State University, as part of a study published in *Developmental Psychology*.

Jealousy can create a downward spiral of mistrust and cause a severe disconnect in a relationship. Constantly dealing with it can be exhausting for both partners.

Some of the best advice for coping with jealousy is the simplest: calm down, take a deep breath or two, and then take an honest look at what is happening. Are you feeling jealous about something that has truly happened or that you have personally witnessed (you saw a photo on Instagram of your girlfriend kissing someone else) or something that you heard about or even just imagined (your boyfriend said he was going to track practice, but you heard someone saw him at the mall with another person)? Before you get upset, make sure there actually is something to be upset about.

Talking Yourself Down

Another key to lessening jealousy is being careful of what you allow that critical inner voice to say to you. It often works to increase your self-doubt and erode your self-confidence by telling you what terrible things your partner might be doing or saying or how unacceptable you are as a partner. Always keep in mind that the root of jealousy is the fear of being replaced. If you feel inadequate or insecure, it will make sense for someone to replace you.

Dr. Lisa Firestone writes for *Psych Alive,* "Remember that your critical inner voice is not a reflection of reality. Don't act on what this voice tells you." She further recommends that you fight back against that voice by writing down the negative thoughts your inner voice keeps saying, but by writing about

Jealousy can affect how you look at the innocent behavior of a partner with others. Not every instance of physical contact should be interpreted as blatant flirtation.

them in second person, as "you" statements. Then, write positive responses to those statements in first person, as "I" statements. "In response to a thought like, 'You're such an idiot,'" says Firestone, "you could write, 'I may struggle at times, but I am smart and competent in many ways.'" If your inner voice says, "You're so unattractive, of course your boyfriend is looking at other girls," you could respond with, "I am a pretty girl and my boyfriend knows this." This exercise can help you see how critical and hostile your inner voice can be—and how to respond to it in ways to make it go away.

Dr. Dion Metzger, in her interview with the author, reminds young people that the first step is lessening their feelings of jealousy is to feel comfortable in their own skin. "Know your value, and be appreciative of what you have now. Focus and write down what you're happy about, or good at, or what you appreciate about yourself. When you

Writing down your feelings and thoughts can help you work through them, and even provide you with realizations about yourself and your relationship.

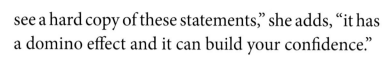

see a hard copy of these statements," she adds, "it has a domino effect and it can build your confidence."

Avoid Playing Games

Just as it is important not to let jealousy become a problem in your relationships, it is also a big mistake to play the type of games with your partner that can result in jealousy. For example, do not flirt with other people when you are in a committed relationship. You might think it is fun to flirt while your partner is watching from afar—maybe you think it would help him or her to appreciate you more. Sadly, this is rarely true. Instead, it tends to cause your partner to feel vulnerable and inadequate.

The same is true if you go on and on about how attractive another person is—whether it's a new student in school, a coworker, or a celebrity. If you keep pointing out how tall and muscular he is or how curvy and athletic she is, your partner may be flooded with insecurity. Finally, do not spend time discussing the wonders of your ex-girlfriend or boyfriend. (After all, you are talking about your ex, so how can he or she be all that great?) Again, this will most likely damage your partner's self-esteem—not something you should want to do to anyone you care about.

Anger is a common response to feeling jealous. It is a powerful defense mechanism, too. It is also a sign that it is time to talk things out.

Time to Communicate

While there is quite a bit you can do to lessen the feelings of jealousy you are experiencing, there is one thing you need to do, but cannot do alone: honestly communicate your feelings to your partner. Explain that you feel jealous whenever he/she _____ (fill in the blank with whatever behavior gets to you, such as "doesn't answer my texts," "talks with the cute new kid at school," etc.). Just discussing these behaviors and how they make you feel may be enough to clear up the issue. Sharing your emotions is also a way to bring the two of you closer and build the trust you have in each other.

A Little Separateness

Another way to protect yourself from being impacted by jealousy is keeping a little distance between you and your partner. As author Kahlil Gibran once wrote, "Let there be spaces in your togetherness." Remember that you are each separate individuals, with your own likes, dislikes, flaws, skills, hobbies, and personalities. Dr. Daniel Siegel, author and clinical professor

Sometimes one of the best ways to process your jealousy is to get away from your partner and talk things out with friends who can provide helpful insights.

of psychiatry at UCLA School of Medicine told *Psychology Today* that the goal of a relationship should be to "make a fruit salad and not a smoothie."

To be a couple, then, should not necessarily mean each partner has to give up his or her own individuality. This is especially true for adolescents and teenagers, who are trying to figure out who they are, often with much struggle and sometimes in an emotionally difficult fashion. Ultimately, being whole within oneself will help anyone have a healthier relationship with another.

If you find that you keep obsessing over the fact that you might lose your partner, try this experiment and see what you can learn from it. Therapist Mark Tyrrell suggests on his website, Uncommon Help, "Write down 10 positive ways you'd like to respond (if you lost your partner) and how you'd build your life up even better if this relationship were to end. Fear is much greater when we feel that 'all our eggs are in one basket.'" He adds, "Don't build your whole life around any one person."

Think, Don't Act

As upset as jealousy may make you feel, it is absolutely essential that you keep a cap on the emotion so you do not physically act on it. Studies have shown that jealousy, like anger, can result in dangerous mistakes. Insecurities can lead to counterproductive, destructive, abusive, and sometimes even dangerous behaviors. Being jealous or possessive can hurt one's partner, and it can poison one's own experiences, too. You can tell you have entered the danger zone when you find yourself sneaking around, eavesdropping on conversations, or looking through text messages, emails, records of online chats, or social media activities. For example, it's one thing to scroll through someone's profile on Facebook or another platform to catch up informally and look at some pictures. But doing it obsessively or to intentionally look for something to get jealous over is obviously going too far. Working to nip such activities and behaviors before they really begin can even make you feel more in control and confident. In addition, that shows that you can be trustworthy and confident in your relationships.

Dr. Robert Leahy agrees with the importance of not acting out when feeling jealous. "Just as there is a difference between feeling angry and acting in a hostile way, there is a difference between feeling jealous and acting on your jealousy," he writes in *Psychology Today*. Jealous behavior can jeopardize one's relationship entirely. Such behavior may include repeatedly accusing someone of cheating or secretly liking another, or flirting with someone else. It can also mean continually seeking reassurance from a partner. A jealous partner may constantly pout and act out. Many of these behaviors can become annoying, stifling, and downright infuriating over time.

When Things Go Too Far

A 2005 study from Pennsylvania State University showed that jealousy is not only linked to low self-esteem but also to aggression. This means a jealous person can easily become an aggressive person. How do you know if your partner's jealousy is actually a serious problem? It can be hard to tell. Dr. Dion Metzger says, "Jealousy is a human reflex, a natural emotion, but when it starts to consume you, and become all you can think about, those are major red flags." Metzger believes that jealousy is often aggravated by today's focus on social media. "Feelings of jealousy are often out in the open. Young people can see it online—and so can everyone else. Everything is on display."

Love or Control?

It can be very hard to recognize when you are in a damaging relationship. Your friends and family might have noticed it happening already and tried to talk to you about it, but you think they're wrong. Your partner loves you so much that he wants to control what you do, right? Isn't that a sign that he cares? He or she just wants to spend more time with you and have more of your attention, right?

Check out the list below, adapted from the website Love: The Good, the Bad and the Ugly and see what you learn about your relationship. Answer honestly—if not, you are only lying to yourself.

My partner . . .	Always	Sometimes	Never
Seems to like me for who I am.			
Won't let me talk to other guys/girls.			
Checks up on what I do, where I go, or whom I've been talking to.			
Tries to stop me from spending time with my friends or family.			
Makes me feel like I have to watch what I do or say.			
Is OK if I say no to something (including sex).			
Is happy that I make my own decisions about my life.			
Puts me down or humiliates me.			

My partner . . .	Always	Sometimes	Never
Has been aggressive or violent.			
Tries to work out arguments by compromising or talking.			
Has pressured, forced, or tricked me into doing unwanted sexual things.			
Has acted in ways that have scared or hurt me.			
Is happy for me to hang out with friends, without him/her there also.			
Has threatened to hurt me or kill him/herself if I end the relationship.			
Makes me feel scared to disagree or to say no to things.			

What are some of the signs that you or your partner is becoming dangerously jealous? Ask yourself: Are you always trying to soothe your partner's feelings? Answer his or her questions? Explain your actions? The following are some of the most common indications that your partner's jealousy has turned into a true problem in your relationship:

- Demonstrating aggressive behavior, including hitting, slapping, pushing, shaking, smacking, kicking, punching, or grabbing
- Using verbal abuse in anger, such as yelling, swearing, and name calling

- Trying to control your actions, activities, choice of clothing, and friends
- Being possessive of your time, so you can't spend it with friends or family
- Not allowing you to make a decision on your own
- Stalking your social media sites, text messages, emails, and phone calls
- Accusing you of being unfaithful without providing any evidence
- Getting mad at you over little issues
- Humiliating you or making you feel unworthy
- Drilling you with questions about where you have been, who you were with, and other details whenever you are not with him or her
- Demanding you answer all of his or her phone calls and texts immediately
- Criticizing your friends and trying to drive a wedge between you and them
- Tagging along whenever you try to go somewhere with others
- Threatening to harm you or himself or herself if you end the relationship

As Kay Ireland writes in *Modern Mom*, "A healthy relationship is built upon a high degree of mutual trust and respect . . . Relationships should never be isolating or make you feel as though you need to apologize for your normal behavior."

Jealousy is a normal, human emotion, and it is healthy to allow yourself to feel it. Some people even get a charge or thrill from making partners jealous. Other partners consider inspiring jealousy in their significant others to mean that they are valued. But there are definite limits to what constitutes healthy jealousy. If you can joke around about being jealous with your partner, that is probably a good sign.

However, when jealousy makes day-to-day living difficult, when it harms your connection to your partner, or when you spend more time trying to keep your relationship safe than you do just enjoying it, something is wrong. Even in cases where things do not go off the rails in a scary way, a jealous partner can make for exhausting company. This can even be multiplied many times over if two individuals prone to jealousy end up dating each other. What should be an enjoyable time instead becomes a series of jealous games one or both partners play with each other. Young people should tame the green-eyed monster before it has the chance to get loose and sabotage their current relationship—and their future relationships as well.

Myths & FACTS

Myth: Jealousy is never a positive emotion in a relationship, only negative.

Fact: A little bit of jealousy can sometimes be a positive thing. This is true if it helps partners negotiate boundaries in a relationship, for example. Some jealousy, handled by talking openly, can help solidify a bond.

Myth: All breakups are unpleasant and create negative feelings for both people involved..

Fact: There are breakups that are done mutually and maturely so that neither person is feeling hurt, angry, or depressed. They may not be easy, but they are possible if both people work on it.

Myth: Getting over a breakup is typically quick and easy for most teens.

Fact: It can take time for both partners to recover from a breakup, even the person who initiates it.

CHAPTER THREE

Breaking Up Is Hard to Do

Nicole lay curled up on her bed, crying as if it were the end of the world. She had just broken up with her boyfriend of two years. Even though he had done it kindly, and even though she knew it was the best thing for both of them, it still hurt like nothing else she had ever experienced. What would she do with herself now? Would she ever fall in love again? Had she made a mistake in agreeing to this breakup? Should she call him up and suggest they try again? How was she going to make it through the rest of the day, let alone the rest of her life?

It is understandable why Nicole felt this awful. Breaking up is one of the most painful events anyone can go through, and for teens, who tend to be low on experience and high on emotions and hormones, it can be absolutely overwhelming. "For young people, a breakup is

The end of a relationship, especially one that has lasted a long time, is traumatic for almost everyone, regardless of who initiated it.

devastating, the end of the world," says Dr. Dion Metzger. "It is because that relationship was your [whole] world." It can seem so because one has put so much time and effort into the person and the relationship itself. Breaking up can hit some people pretty hard, even affecting their sleep patterns, appetite, and other normal daily functions.

There is absolutely no question about it. Whether you are the one initiating the breakup or the one who is being broken up with, it hurts. It hurts terribly. Helen Fisher, an anthropologist at Rutgers University, explains to *Psychology Today* writer Elizabeth Svoboda one reason the end of a relationship is so incredibly painful: "Because our brains are wired from the beginning for bonding, breakups batter us biologically. Initially, everyone reacts to rejection like a drug user going through withdrawal." Fisher, along with UCLA psychologist Naomi Eisenberger, have found that after a breakup, thinking about your partner triggers the same parts of the brain that are activated when you feel physical pain and distress. Some of these reactions may even be evolutionary in nature. Early humans relied on tight social networks in often harsh environments, and a sense that relationships have value and should not be broken off lightly may have had a hand in humans developing such reactions to separation and breakups.

The Biggest Breaking Up Mistakes

Breaking up is difficult in the best of circumstances, but there are some common mistakes that can make it much worse. Here are some tips to help ensure you will not add fuel to an already painful fire.

- Always break up face to face. Texting, calling, and emailing may feel easier, but they are the cheap way out. Show respect and integrity by doing it in person. "Humans evolved to communicate face to face, which provides some built-in consolations," writes Elizabeth Svoboda for *Psychology Today*. "We may experience many nonverbal clues that reassure us of our essential lovability—the quick touch on the arm that says you're still valued even as the relationship ends. Anything less than face-to-face sends a distressing message: 'You don't matter.'"

- Do not argue about issues in your relationship. There is no point to it. Avoid making the other person feel bad, if at all possible. Simply conveying that he or she is not the right one for you is a better tactic.

- If you are the one being dumped, do not beg your partner to reconsider or give you another chance. Accept the decision and hold your head high—at least until your ex cannot see you anymore. Then you can cry, scream, or swear.

- Don't announce your breakup online or change your Facebook relationship status before telling your partner. Don't text or email your friends first either. It is rude to broadcast the breakup to the world when one partner does not even know it has occurred yet.

- Remember that you will likely keep running into this person at school, at work, or just around, so be kind and act honorably, whether you are the "dumper" or "dumpee." Consider how much better it will feel in a year, or five, when looking back at how well such a difficult situation was handled.

Reasons Behind the Breakup

Chances are the relationships you will have as a teen will not last. (Of course, there are exceptions! "High school sweethearts" still do get married—and stay married—every day.) Why do these relationships not last as long, as a general rule, than adult relationships? There are a number of reasons.

Your teen years are a huge time of change for you. Your thoughts, ideas, preferences, and personality are constantly shifting. In part, this is due to a changing brain. Dr. Robert Hedaya, clinical professor of psychiatry at Georgetown University told *Psychology Today* that adolescents' brains are still developing, and this process means all of their emotional responses and actions are in flux, never quite the same from day to day. "During the teen years," says Hedaya, "under the influence of massive new hormonal

Whether a breakup was mutual or one sided, both parties need to be prepared to eventually run into their ex-partner at school or in other places they commonly gather.

messages, as well as current needs and experiences, the teenager's brain is being reshaped, and reconstructed . . . It's a massive construction project, unlike anything that occurs at any other time in life." Clearly, this makes maintaining a relationship based on feelings pretty challenging.

Another reason young couples break up is from outside pressure. It might be from friends who don't like your partner or just wish you had more free time to spend with them. It might be from your parents who worry that your relationship is not healthy for you or see trouble ahead and urge you to end the connection.

Some breakups happen because one of the two people in the relationship ends up being attracted to someone else. One person may even cheat on the other and date or be intimate with another person secretly. While multiple partners are usually accepted in open relationships, the betrayal can cause a great deal of stress in one-on-one relationships.

Exiting Abusive Relationships

Finally, some teens break up because of abuse—an excellent reason to end a relationship immediately. According to *Teens Health*, one in eleven high school students report being physically hurt by a partner. When you are in a relationship with someone who is emotionally and/or physically abusive, it is time to

One partner might initiate a breakup if he or she has become interested in another potential partner. It is usually a sign to move on if you find yourself flirting with others, especially secretly.

end it, even if it means asking for help from family, a friend, or other adult.

The most important thing to consider when suffering through an abusive relationship is looking out for one's own safety, no matter how attached one feels to the other person. A partner might feel sorry for the other person or have convinced himself or herself that the abusive partner will somehow change his or her ways and stop being abusive. This can be the case for those who are emotionally abusive, physically abusive, or both. Often the two go hand in hand.

In getting out of an abusive relationship, one's own safety is the most important consideration. Cutting off all ties is usually the best option, even if you must do so delicately and strategically. This includes blocking the person from calling or texting and from any and all points of social media connection.

Do not be afraid to consult with parents, other responsible adults, teachers, guidance counselors, or even law enforcement if necessary. Another good idea is to ask a friend to accompany you to places where you may encounter an ex. The support of friends and family is also crucial to building back one's self-confidence and making you ready one day to enter a new relationship with a person who is caring, respectful, and not abusive.

Breakup Etiquette

When you're in the middle of a breakup, it can be hard to remember to be kind and patient, but it is also very important. In today's world of electronic communication, it can feel much easier to rely on texts, calls, and emails to deliver the bad news, and that is just what some teens do. In one survey, as reported in *Psychology Today*, 24 percent of respondents between the ages of thirteen and seventeen said it was completely OK to break up with someone via text—and 26 percent admitted to doing so.

Obviously, it feels less stressful to text. You don't have to see the tears or the hurt on your partner's face. You won't be interrupted. Some people handle face-to-face tension or disagreement better than others. Many sensitive adolescents and teenagers like to avoid conflict and hurting others. They do not like to see the consequence of their actions. Texting also helps young people cope with the situation and allows them to move forward with ending the relationship.

The same is true for leaving a voicemail or sending an email or a private message via social media. It is somewhat cowardly and even disrespectful to break up in this manner, especially if the relationship was a close or intense one. That very seriousness and closeness may make it that much more of a scary proposition to approach

Those going through a breakup often feel like they are alone in their experience. It is important to remember that everyone goes through such experiences and feels such emotions.

a partner in person and break such bad news.

While it may be easier to use text, many people will agree that it is not the honorable way to end a relationship. "It's always been hard to break up with someone face to face," Stanford University sociologist and author Clifford Nass told *Psychology Today*, "but lack of social skills makes it harder. And we're learning fewer and fewer social skills."

Another recent and unfortunate technique is is "ghosting." This is the practice of breaking off all communication with a partner without any warning whatsoever and completely ignoring the person. This is a cruel and misguided tactic and should be avoided.

Consider breaking up with someone in person,

however, over any other manner of communication, as long as it feels safe to do so. Think about the other person's feelings and how you yourself would feel if you heard from a boyfriend or girlfriend—especially all of a sudden—that he or she was cutting off ties. Being broken up with remotely can leave the person who is dumped feeling adrift in relationship limbo. He or she may lack the closure needed to move on. It is also in your interest to break up in person because then it may be more definitive and convincing for the other person to move on, rather than hang on to the pointless hope of somehow getting back together.

Keeping Things Smooth

Clearly, breaking up in person is the most respectful way to end a relationship. What else can you do to make sure it goes as painlessly as possible? First, make sure of your decision before you initiate it. This is not the time to be wishy-washy and easily dissuaded. This is not a negotiation. Planning out what to say ahead of time and thinking about how the other person will most likely react can help you prepare effectively.

It may be a good idea to throw out hints in conversation beforehand, before the actual meeting. Of course, it depends on the people involved. Some people may feel more hurt by the uncertainty and

If you are initiating the breakup, remember the adage of "Do unto others as you would have them do unto you." Be firm and clear but kind.

racing thoughts that they are sure to endure. Saying "we need to talk" and making a plan to do so may help or hurt the situation, depending on the person. Also keep in mind that even if you are more than ready for this breakup, your partner may be devastated. With that in mind, make sure you know how you will react if your ex begins yelling or breaks down in tears. Be ready to provide sympathy but without backtracking or giving the now ex-partner any hope of reconnecting.

Second, choose a good time and place. Right in the middle of the cafeteria in front of everyone is not a great choice. Just before taking a test, going to work, or heading out to participate in a performance are not good options either. Choose somewhere private, quiet, and comfortable (but safe). It is common for at least one of you to feel some pretty strong emotions, and experiencing that in front of a crowd or when you need to concentrate is tough. In addition, if possible, try to avoid breaking up with someone on his or her birthday or during other special occasions or milestones.

Third, "try to stay away from name calling, blame or comparisons," advises Dr. Dion Metzger. "You want to leave on the best possible terms. Be as direct as possible, but also as kind as you can." This isn't the time to rehash old conflicts and argue about who was right and who was wrong. Just deliver the message and stick to it.

Open but Still Jealous?

How can jealousy play a part in open relationships? If partners have agreed to let each other date other people, doesn't that solve the issue of jealousy? You might feel disappointed in yourself or your partner if either of you start struggling with this emotion. Wendy-O Matik, author of *Redefining Our Relationships: Guidelines for Responsible Open Relationships*, told the Your Tango website, "People in non-monogamous relationships can feel pressured to deny or bury their jealousy just because they think it's wrong to feel that way. Instead, we should say, 'Yep, I'm jealous, and it feels really awful.' Denying it, of course, will just make it get worse."

Open relationships can be tricky, so it is important that you communicate well and discuss what rules or boundaries you want in place. Your limits to what feels okay may not match up with your partner's, for example. Maybe you don't want to know about anyone else the other person is dating—or maybe you want to meet him or her? Perhaps you don't mind if your partner dates others, but not anyone going to the same school as you? As Matik puts it, "If guidelines are laid down in the beginning, there's less opportunity to accidentally snag a jealousy trip wire."

If there is anything close to an ideal breakup, it should include acceptance of the situation by both parties, with the least amount of psychological pain involved. A relationship should be ended definitively and with honor. Neither person should walk away believing they have been disrespected. Of course, in the real world, many of these criteria are often not met, and even relatively easy breakups can cause pain and resentment.

The TeensHealth website recommends that you follow this pattern for breaking up kindly:

1. Tell the person that you want to talk about something important.
2. Begin by focusing on something you like or appreciate about the other person. ("I am glad we have had the chance to get to know each other. I love your sense of humor." Or, "I

Breaking up is often an intense experience for anyone, so it is advised that people do it carefully, in private (if it is safe to do so), and with kindness.

learned so much about myself being with you. I won't ever forget this time in our lives.")

3. Point out (without any blame) what you feel is not working in the relationship or the reason you think things would be better if you broke up. ("We spend so much time arguing" or "I need more time to focus on school and my family.")

4. Clearly state you want to break up—don't be vague. You are not helping the situation by trying to say it subtly.

5. Say you are sorry if this is hurtful. Be sincere.

6. Say something kind or positive. ("You are incredible, and I know you won't have any trouble finding someone you deserve.")

7. Listen to the other person patiently and kindly.

8. Give that person the chance to react as he or she needs to.

A Storm of Feelings

Once the breakup is over, it is time to deal with the emotions it carries along with it. These feelings can be overwhelming and hard to cope with for many teens. Colie Taico, a licensed clinical social worker and psychotherapist, notes, "The loss of a relationship can bring on a tsunami of feelings ranging from denial to anger. While the emotions feel intense, try to remember that it will pass and that you're not alone. Every human experiences loss and grief in their lifetimes at some point."

It is essential that, as you grieve the end of a relationship, you fight to not let it damage your self-respect and confidence. That will only make the pain last longer. Even situations in which relationships actually haven't developed—like partners shopping around for companionship on online dating sites and apps—can spark feelings of rejection and affect one's self-confidence. It is perhaps unsurprising that people with lower self-esteem often take rejection more harshly than others. They often blame themselves for the rejection, rather than just chalking it up to normal incompatibility or simply recognizing that it did not work out. Even those with high self-esteem are not immune to self-doubt in the face of rejection. But they tend to keep seeing themselves in a relatively positive light, unlike their peers who take rejection extremely personally.

It is common to experience a rush of emotions during and following a breakup, especially if an argument led to the breakup, or if the breakup came seemingly out of the blue. Some of the most common reactions might include anger, hopelessness, desperation, anxiety, and a generalized depression. If you are the one that ended it, you might be feeling guilt, too. A recent study in the *Journal of Abnormal*

Psychology noted that teenagers in particular were prone to major depression following a romantic breakup. Another notable reaction includes shutting down emotionally, which serves as a defense mechanism.

The negative feelings that often arise after a breakup may not be limited to one's emotions. Many young people experience physical symptoms—even actual pain and physical afflictions. These may include headaches or aches throughout the body. Some of this may happen due to the hormones that flood the body in stressful situations, including adrenaline, which increases blood circulation, breathing, and other processes. People react differently to a breakup. Some may be anxious or excitable and can experience restlessness. Others become more withdrawn and sleep away their days.

For some young people, the roller-coaster of emotions and thoughts that accompany a breakup may be one of the most intense experiences of their lives.

65

After a breakup, life can be really difficult. You might feel sad and lonely. You might not want to do anything but sit in your room and listen to sad songs or wallow in other melancholy or depressing art. That may be just what you need for the first few days. In fact, it is good to feel what you need to in order to come to terms with a situation. But eventually it will be time to pick yourself up off the ground, or out of bed, and move on.

Getting Back Up After the Fall

The breakup is over. The avalanche of emotions has buried you for days—or weeks—or longer. Everyone is telling you it is time to move on, get over it, buck up, move forward—just get back up. Sounds great, but how can you manage it? Right now, it seems impossible.

It helps to realize that, like with any other major loss in life, you are bound to go through phases of emotions. How long each one lasts depends on the person, but everyone tends to experience them. When the breakup initially happens, you will most likely go through a period of shock and devastation. Your world has drastically changed. Your heart is hurt. Your self-confidence is shaken. You may feel extra sensitive or completely numb.

Part of denial may include going over old emails or social media posts in an attempt to figure out how to get the person back.

Denial

Next, you may hit a wall of denial. You didn't break up. You're just putting the relationship on pause for a while. You'll be back together soon, right? Such doubts may even plague a partner who initiates the breakup, especially if he or she was torn about whether to go through with it to begin with. Denial about the situation can serve as a coping mechanism. It gives the person some time to process the new reality, outside of the relationship. People may feel foolish later, for not accepting things as quickly as they feel they should have, but it is a perfectly natural reaction to have.

Denial is often followed up by a period of self-doubt. Why didn't you try harder? You may have irrational thoughts rooted in low self-esteem. You should have lost those ten pounds. You should have spent more time with her. You should have been a better partner in one way or another. These thoughts can be upsetting and

While negative emotions are perfectly normal following a breakup, they should never cross over into hurting yourself or others. Reach out to someone if you find you are having especially dark thoughts.

depressing, and while they are normal to experience, if you linger on them too long, your self-esteem is going to suffer.

For many young people, denial is followed by a period of anger. This isn't fair! Your ex was so mean! You'll show him. During this phase, you might be tempted to get revenge or do something stupid or impulsive. It's often a time of rash decisions. Allow yourself to feel the anger, but find healthy ways to act on it.

Eventually, you should reach a place of accepting the breakup and feeling relatively calm about it. Dr. Dion Metzger advises, "Remember—the sun will come out tomorrow. Breaking up is a very maturing experience. It is not something that is a quick fix or something you could necessarily control. Realize that some people in your life are only meant to be chapters," she adds. "One day you will be grateful because this breakup will show you that you can recover from what feels like the end of the world. It introduces you to the idea that you will get through."

Staying Positive

For years, psychologists, counselors, and other therapists have known that positive affirmations can help a person recover from a traumatic experience. Beyond being simply self-help clichés, you can think of affirmation as including ways to transform your subconscious thoughts, internalize positive thoughts and self-image, and situate your place in the world in an optimistic light.

Affirmations are statements that encourage, reassure, and inspire people. Typically they are written in the first person and present tense. They are always positive statements (e.g., "I will control what I eat" rather than "I will not eat as much") and usually involve emotions. Some people write these affirmations on paper and read them (aloud) daily. Others put them on cards and post them where they can see them daily, such as the bathroom mirror or next to their bed. Here are some of the best statements one can use when recovering from a breakup:

- My life is full of possibility.
- I can easily find someone else to love.
- I can move on with my life.
- I am in control of my emotions.
- My heart heals more each day.

- I am strong and valuable and have much to offer the world.
- I let go of the pain from my last relationship.
- I am worthy of being loved for who I am.
- I attract wonderful, loving, positive people into my life.
- All things are unfolding are they are supposed to.

Routes to Recovery

Sadly, there is no magic pill or single method to getting over the pain of a breakup. It takes time—often months—to feel like you've gotten past it. In the meantime, there are a number of ways to make you either temporarily forget the pain or, at least, buffer it a bit.

Start by allowing yourself to feel miserable. Cry, yell, punch your pillow, or scream. You have every right to be sad and upset. Trying to ignore it or suppress it will only make you feel worse. Contrary to what you may think, there is absolutely no shame in tears. You opened your heart to someone, made yourself vulnerable, and got hurt.

Breakups can be tough, and this includes the often intense emotions that well up within us during

Following a breakup is one of the best times to start a new hobby or return to an old one. Fill your time with an activity that makes you smile and relax.

and after breaking up. Despite the longtime taboo against guys showing too much emotion, both males and females can benefit from crying it out. No one has to see you do it, though it can certainly be helpful if you find a shoulder to cry on. That includes a parental shoulder, a sibling's, or that of a close friend. For others, just crying in private (for example, into a pillow in bed at night) can make you feel much better. You can even watch sappy movies or read books that help you cry for a different reason.

There is no doubt that this is a very emotional time for you. Recognizing, validating, and expressing those emotions is healthy. There are also ways for you to channel sadness and anger into constructive activities. For example, clean your room to release some energy. This can also kill two birds with one stone, so to speak—that is, it is a good time to remove any of your ex's belongings or anything that reminds you of the person. Repaint, rearrange, or reorganize everything so it feels fresh and new. It will serve as a

Therapy or counseling after a breakup can be helpful. This is especially true for young people who already have other emotional or psychological issues.

reminder and a marker for a new phase of life. As you're cleaning and moving furniture around, try listening to your favorite music loud. The physical activity can help get your blood going and improve your mood, too.

Another great way to express your emotions in a safe and productive way is to start some type of exercise. Ride your bike, take up running, or join a gym or club. At the very least, get at least thirty minutes of exercise at least three times a week, and much more if you have the time and energy. You will feel better about yourself and the situation, and you will be able to think more clearly about it.

You might consider volunteering within your community also. Helping others is a healthy way of getting over (or at least temporarily ignoring) your sadness and increasing your self-esteem. It encourages you to interact with others and possibly even make new friends.

Next, be extra kind and gentle to yourself. Watch your favorite movies. Snack on your favorite foods (try

Writing can be highly therapeutic. If you already have a journal, or regularly write down your thoughts, doing so about a breakup can help bring some perspective and relieve some stress.

to avoid negative behaviors like bingeing, however!). Get a little extra sleep if you need it. Spend time with friends and family who love you and understand what you are going through. Find ways to appreciate your newfound freedom and the ability to do what you want with your free time without worrying about annoying, angering, or disappointing a partner.

Writing Away the Pain

If you enjoy writing, take time to write out your feelings and thoughts. This isn't going to be graded or read by anyone else, so swear, rant, ask questions, whatever feels most helpful. Just putting the thoughts on paper (or a keyboard) helps release them from your mind. This is especially true for feelings of anger, disappointment, and betrayal. Letting these emotions fester within yourself only compounds mild depression. You can write down your private thoughts by hand in a journal.

Online Healing Help

If you are feeling confessional, you can start a blog or Tumblr and express your feelings there. You can write anonymously, or under assumed names, or pseudonyms. On blogs and on social media accounts, you can get affirmation, encouragement, and support from friends or even concerned strangers who can relate to your feelings.

Of course, be considerate of the feelings of your ex and of his or her privacy. It is imperative that you leave out identifying information. This is especially true if you are going to relate intimate details about your relationship. Even if certain facts are true to life, your writing can embarrass a partner and even affect his or her reputation, both online and off. Thoughtless blogging or posting can end up with your partner becoming the victim of online or physical harassment and could even cost him or her a job or get him or her kicked out of school. The same may happen to you.

Another pitfall could be compromising your own privacy or safety and attracting unwanted attention from potential stalkers or online predators. Forums for young people suffering emotional issues or problems can be a great place to blow off steam. But they might also attract strangers with unsavory intentions, including manipulative people who pretend to sympathize but are actually looking for vulnerable victims to ensnare.

Loved Ones: There for You

Sharing what you are feeling can help lessen the pain, so reach out to your family and friends. Even if you need some time alone, think about how some company might eventually cheer you up, while providing someone to bounce your feelings off. Pick up the phone and call someone you trust to listen with love and patience. One study, as reported by PR Newswire, revealed that the top eight people who get called following a breakup include the following, with their accompanying percentages: a female friend (27 percent); mother (17 percent); a sibling (10 percent); a male friend (10 percent); father (2 percent); the recent ex (2 percent); and a past ex (1 percent).

Help from a Pro

While family and friends can help you deal with all you are experiencing, if you are struggling with intense depression, feelings of hopelessness or despair, or suicidal thoughts, it is time to call in extra help. Let a trusted adult know that you need help so you can see a professional, or seek one out yourself.

A professional ear can often be helpful, whether it is a psychologist, psychiatrist, therapist, or other mental health professional. It can truly help to talk out your feelings and thoughts since these specialists have years of training and experience helping people suffering through relationship problems and breakups.

Another person to possibly consult, for those who are religious or have been raised in a particular faith, is a member of the clergy. A priest, rabbi, imam, or other local faith leader or influential member of one's temple or church can be very insightful and helpful. Even beyond a religious perspective, many clergy are experienced in helping youth navigate the often turbulent waters of youthful heartache and heartbreak.

Other Options

What are other ways to make this time of life a little easier? Now that you have more free time, consider exploring a new hobby. Melanie Haiken, writing for *HealthDay*, advises, "If you've healed enough to venture out of your routine, consider taking a class or otherwise nurturing your creativity. If there's something you've always wanted to learn how to do, now may be a good time to try."

A breakup might free up your time to do things you have put off doing or may have been unable to do, including catching up on reading, especially if a stressful relationship was time-consuming.

There is another step to helping yourself recover from a breakup, but it can be a tough one: stay away from your ex as much as possible. Erase those emails and delete those text messages. Gather up belongings and return them through a friend. Reaching out to your old partner can easily rekindle your feelings, give you false hope, and eliminate any of the progress you have made. This is true for both in-person and online encounters. If you can do it, stay away from social media for a while. Unplugging from social media for a time, or at least dramatically limiting usage, is good advice for any young person in the modern era, but especially for someone requiring time to think, escape, and self-heal.

The expression "time heals all wounds" certainly applies when it comes to breakups. As time passes, the pain will begin to lessen little by little, your feelings will begin to moderate a bit, and slowly the clouds will clear and you will be able to see the sunshine and blue sky around you once again. Just hang in there, and realize all you have learned.

10 Great Questions to Ask a Counselor

1. Is it normal to feel jealous of my partner?

2. Is jealousy always a negative emotion to have?

3. What should I do when I feel anger and jealousy?

4. Are there ways to stop these feelings of jealousy?

5. How can I recognize when jealousy has gone too far?

6. How long does it take to recover from a breakup?

7. What can I do to keep myself busy after the breakup?

8. Is it natural to cry every day after a breakup?

9. How do I let go of the pain and anger I feel about the relationship?

10. What are ways I can forgive myself and/or my partner and move forward?

CHAPTER FIVE

Life Lessons Learned

Have you ever noticed that the biggest lessons you have learned about life tended to come from the most difficult experiences? When life is going right for you, it is easy to float along and enjoy it. Life is easy and simple. But when you encounter a problem, from a lousy grade to a sick friend to a potential breakup, that is when you learn more about yourself and the world. Eleanor Roosevelt once said, "A woman is like a tea bag; you can't tell how strong she is until she is in hot water." This could be said about any teen going through a breakup. You may not realize how tough and resilient you are until you experience heartbreak. As *Teen Vogue* writer Marissa Miller points out, "And so this [breaking up] is just another one of those things in life for which there is no workaround: You can't go over it, you can't go under it, you've got to go through it. And once you have, you'll be stronger for it."

Breaking Up by the Numbers

Multiple studies and research has been done on the science of breakups. Using some of this data, information designers David McCandless and Lee Byron presented some fascinating statistics to the A Plus website.

(continued on the next page)

The holidays can be stressful for some, and some of this stress may come from thinking hard about whether continuing with an iffy relationship is the right way forward or not.

(continued from the previous page)

The majority of breakups occur over spring break (February/March), spike again around April Fool's Day, and finally peak during the winter holiday season (from November through December).

While almost half of all breakups are still done in person, 30 percent happen over the phone, 14 percent over instant message, 5 percent on Facebook, and 4 percent over email.

About 3.5 percent of breakups occur because parents or friends do not approve of the partner.

A teenager might look back, even from the more experienced perspective of adulthood years later, and reflect on what he or she learned from a painful breakup. Such experiences provide new standards and guidelines about what someone should expect from a healthy relationship and how to figure out when a normal one has entered unhealthy territory. It can help one be a better partner in future situations and give someone the strength to demand to be treated with care.

Breakups can also jump-start other periods in your life. When you need to get your head together after a breakup, life-changing experiences like traveling, volunteering, entering a new job, and

Before or during a breakup, things might seem grim. However, once you get through it, you will soon feel like your old self again and be able to enjoy life.

other journeys in life can be just the thing.

It can be hard to realize that you are learning essential life lessons while immersed in the pain of a breakup. It is like hearing about a favorite dish while sick with a bad case of the stomach flu. You just are not interested right now. But just as that favorite dish can be enjoyed at some point in the future, one day it will become apparent that breaking up provided some of the most useful and important life lessons imaginable.

All About You

Reflecting back on the relationship that has ended can often help you figure out what went wrong and what you want to change the next time you fall in love. The only way to really learn how to have a relationship is to actually experience one, with all the stumbles, breakups, and rebounds it entails. If you do not try to learn from what you have experienced,

When to jump back into the dating game may vary greatly depending on your personality. But once the time is right, you will certainly have the chance to build something with someone new.

you are likely destined to repeat it again and again.

Once you have enough distance from your breakup, consider making a list of things about your ex you really liked (he made me laugh, she liked to read just as much as I do, he had great hair, etc.) and what you most definitely did not like (she was always late, he thought my hobbies were stupid, she looked at other guys all the time, etc.). That list can help you choose more wisely the next time you get involved with someone. You will know what elements of behavior, personality, and actions are most important to you and which ones you either do not appreciate or do not want in a close romantic relationship.

More Life Lessons

What else can a breakup teach you about life and, more important, about yourself? There are a number of profound lessons. You can learn to enjoy time alone, for example. It may

Beyond simply getting over a bad relationship and a tough breakup, doing so with kindness and respect will equip you to have happy, healthy relationships in the future.

feel lonely and awkward at first, but over time, you will adjust to spending more time by yourself. It can be incredibly comfortable and relaxing to just be you, without worrying about how you look, what you say, or what you want to do—or not do. Enjoying time on your own can be quite empowering and a skill that will follow and help you for the rest of your life.

Do not rush and put pressure on yourself to find another partner right away. Avoid rebounding. Go through what some people refer to as dating detox. As Sara Altschule explains in an article for Bustle, "If you are one of those people who go from relationship to relationship, you might want to consider a 'dating detox.' You can choose however long the detox needs to be. Standing on your own, and learning how to be alone and single is crucial."

By going through such processes, teens can learn to love themselves, outside the boundaries of relationships. Enjoy this time as a single person. People who rely on their relationships to derive their self-worth are almost always going to be disappointed. Instead, get comfortable and content with who you are, on your own. Then take that confidence out into the world.

Going through a really difficult experience like a breakup can also show you how you deal with the stress of loss and grief. As you look back over your

Breakup Books

Need to know that people your age understand exactly what you're going through? Have your friends heard enough of your venting? Pick up a book about breakups and empathize with the characters. Here are a dozen titles to check out at the library, buy at a bookstore, order online, or download:

- *The Sky Is Everywhere*, Jandy Nelson
- *P.S. I Still Love You*, Jenny Han
- *More Happy than Not*, Adam Silvera
- *Why We Broke Up*, Daniel Handler and Maira Kalman
- *The Night We Said Yes*, Lauren Gibaldi
- *The Break-Up Artist*, Philip Siegel
- *The Art of Lainey*, Paula Stokes
- *Starting from Here*, Lisa Jenn Bigelow
- *This Lullaby*, Saran Dessen
- *The Perfectionists*, Sara Shepard
- *We Were Liars*, E. Lockhart
- *Roomies*, Sara Zarr and Tara Altebrando

reactions to the breakup, ask yourself whether you handled it well. What didn't you handle so well? What would you do differently if you could do it all over again? How do you think you will respond to the next breakup in your life, if and when it happens? The answers to these questions will help you get a better perspective on the impact of the relationship on your life, plus a deeper understanding of what you want in the future.

Enduring a loss also reminds you, as impossible as it may seem at one time, that grief over a relationship does eventually end. It is not a lifelong burden you will carry. In fact, chances are, as an adult, you will look back at your relationship—from beginning to end—with a fond smile. Breakups also teach everyone that almost everything in life is temporary and change is inevitable. They also prove to you that you are tougher and stronger than you may have thought (just like Eleanor Roosevelt's tea bag).

Looking to the Future

You've survived the breakup. You've found ways to pick yourself up and move forward. You can still feel the pain and you still think

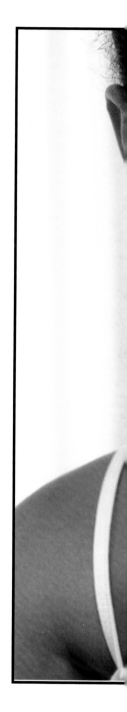

Ultimately, whether you thrive should not depend on your relationship status. Meeting your goals and finding happiness on your own terms are more important.

of your ex, but instead of doing it every few minutes, it happens only a couple of times a day. Soon it will be every other day. You're recovering and the future stretches out in front of you. Now what?

Hopefully, you have a better, clearer idea of what kind of partner you want the next time around. Keep that image in your head, and revamp it as you meet people, learn more about yourself and the world, and cope with your still growing and developing brain. You are so much better equipped to have another relationship now, thanks to the hard lessons the last breakup taught you. With bolstered self-esteem and self-confidence, you are far more likely to connect with someone who is much better suited to you.

Falling in love and being in a relationship are natural and normal parts of growing up. Unfortunately, so is breaking up and ending those relationships, especially if harmful levels of jealousy are involved. Preparing yourself for the emotions that each experience brings is important so that when you go through them, you have the tools not only for your survival but for your happiness as well.

Glossary

adrenaline A hormone released by the human body in response to stress that increases focus, blood circulation, and speeds up breathing.

affirmation A positive statement of support or encouragement.

affliction Something that causes pain or unhappiness.

agitated Describes someone who is anxious, nervous, or disturbed.

anthropologist A person who studies human culture and development.

bile A yellow-green digestive fluid.

conniving Being devious, sneaky, or underhanded.

conscience A person's internal sense of what is right and wrong.

consolation A source of comfort to someone in distress.

covet To intensely desire or want something, including someone who is in a relationship with someone else.

critical inner voice A nagging, negative inner voice that works against one's self-confidence.

empathy The ability to understand how another person feels in a given situation.

erode To wear away or slowly degrade.

ghosting Cutting off all contact with a partner with no warning whatsoever as a means of breaking up.

inevitable Describes a thing, situation, or action that is unavoidable and must eventually be done or occur.

psychotherapist Someone who treats others' mental or emotional disorders, or related bodily illnesses, using psychological means.

suppress To prevent or stop from happening.

vulnerable Open to attack or physical or emotional harm.

For More Information

Advocates for Youth
2000 M Street NW, Suite 750
Washington, DC 20036
(202) 419-3420

Website: http://www.advocatesforyouth.org

Advocates for Youth partners with youth leaders, adult allies, and youth-serving organizations to advocate for policies and champion programs that recognize young people's rights to honest sexual health information; accessible, confidential, and affordable sexual health services; and the resources and opportunities necessary to create sexual health equity for all youth.

Allowance for Good
990 Grove Street, Suite 407
Evanston, IL 60201
(847) 733-0393

Website: http://www.allowanceforgood.org

Allowance for Good aims to empower all youth through the tools of philanthropy to take meaningful action in their world. It connects young people with community service organizations and opportunities, allowing them to donate their time, talents, and money if they have the means.

Canadian Red Cross
(Healthy Youth Dating Relationships)
170 Metcalfe Street
Ottawa, ON K2P 2P2
Canada
(613) 740-1900
Website: http://www.redcross.ca

The Canadian Red Cross's mission is to improve the lives of vulnerable people by mobilizing the power of humanity in Canada and around the world.

Futures Without Violence
100 Montgomery Street, The Presidio
San Francisco, CA 94129
(415) 678-5500
Website: https://www.futureswithoutviolence.org

For more than thirty years, FUTURES has been providing groundbreaking programs, policies, and campaigns that empower individuals and organizations working to end violence against women and children around the world.

Team of Helping Out People Everywhere, Inc. (Team of H.O.P.E.)
PO Box 814523
Hollywood, FL 33081

(305) 930-5997

Website: http://www.theteamofhope.org

Helping Out People Everywhere, Inc., is a 501(c)(3) nonprofit, all-volunteer charitable organization dedicated to the well-being, prosperity, and preservation of communities and families.

Websites

Because of the changing nature of internet links, Rosen Publishing has developed an online list of websites related to the subject of this book. This site is updated regularly. Please use this link to access this list:

http://www.rosenlinks.com/COP/Jealousy

For Further Reading

Acharya, Melysha Jane. *The Breakup Workbook: A Common Sense Guide to Getting Over Your Ex.* New York, NY: BHG Books, 2009.

Atlantic Publishing Company. *Every Young Adult's Breakup Survival Guide: Tips, Tricks & Expert Advice for Recovering.* Ocala, FL: Atlantic Publishing Company, 2015.

Behrendt, Greg, and Amiora Ruotola-Behrendt. *It's Called a Breakup Because It's Broken: The Smart Girl's Break-Up Buddy.* New York, NY: Harmony, 2006.

Day, Emilee. *The Official Teen Survival Guide for Getting Over a Breakup: 22 Steps You Can Take Right Now to Begin Healing.* Create Space, 2016.

DiMarco, Hayley, and Justin Lookadoo. *The Dirt on Breaking Up.* Peabody, MA: Revell, 2008.

Edwards, Daniel. *How to Not Be Jealous: Overcome the Jealousy Which Destroys Your Life and Create a Relationship Based on Trust.* Amazon Digital Services, 2015.

Elliott, Susan J. *Getting Past Your Breakup: How to Turn a Devastating Loss into the Best Thing that Ever Happened to You.* Boston, MA: Da Capo Lifelong Books, 2009.

Price, Sofia. *Jealousy: How to Overcome Jealousy, Insecurity and Trust Issues.* Create Space, 2015.

Simmons, Rachel. *Odd Girl Speaks Out: Girls Write About Bullies, Cliques, Popularity, and Jealousy.* New York, NY: Harcourt, 2004.

Walsh, Marissa. *Not Like I'm Jealous or Anything: The Jealousy Book.* New York, NY: Delacorte Books for Young Readers, 2006.

White, Mandy. *The Jealousy Game: When Jealous Relationships Become Dangerous.* Create Space, 2013.

Bibliography

Berman, Laura. "How Jealous and Possessive Are You?" Everyday Health, November 7, 2012. http://www.everydayhealth.com/sexual-health /dr-laura-berman-how-jealous-and-possessive -are-you.aspx.

Firestone, Lisa. "Critical Inner Voice." Psych Alive. Retrieved October 10, 2016. http://devpsych .psychalive.org/critical-inner-voice.

Firestone, Lisa. "4 Steps to Conquer Your Inner Critic." Psych Alive. Retrieved October 10, 2016. http://www.psychalive.org/4-steps-to-conquer -your-inner-critic.

Firestone, Lisa. "Getting Over Relationship Insecurity." *Huffington Post,* September 25, 2016. http://www.huffingtonpost.com/lisa-firestone /getting-over-relationship_b_8197988.html.

Haiken, Melanie. "Depression after Breakup." *Health Day*, January 20, 2016. https://consumer .healthday.com/encyclopedia/depression-12 /depression-news-176/depression-after-a -breakup-646224.html.

Hedaya, Robert. "The Teenager's Brain." *Psychology Today*, June 3, 2010. https:// www.psychologytoday.com/blog/health -matters/201006/the-teenagers-brain.

Hoyt, Alia. "How Jealousy Works." HowStuffWorks, June 4, 2008. http://science.howstuffworks.com

/life/inside-the-mind/emotions/jealousy.html.

Leahy, Robert. "Jealousy Is a Killer: How to Break Free from Your Jealousy." *Psychology Today*, May 19, 2008. https://www.psychologytoday.com /blog/anxiety-files/200805/jealousy-is-killer -how-break-free-your-jealousy.

Metzger, Dion. Interview with the author. October 11, 2016.

Orr, Nicole. Interview with the author. October 13, 2016.

Scribner, Herb. "How 1 in 3 Teens Handle a Breakup Will Make You Cringe." *Deseret News*, October 1, 2015. http://national.deseretnews .com/article/6266/how-1-in-3-teens-handle-a -breakup-will-make-you-cringe.html.

Scribner, Herb. "Your Brain Holds the Secret to Getting Over a Breakup." *Deseret News*, March 31, 2015. http://national .deseretnews.com/article/3926/your-brain -holds-the-secret-to-getting-over-a-breakup .html#tPuZJQGT0yJi6Djd.99.

Svoboda, Elizabeth. "The Thoroughly Modern Guide to Breakups." *Psychology Today*, January 1, 2011. https://www.psychologytoday.com /articles/201101/the-thoroughly-modern -guide-breakups.

Tyrrell, Mark. "7 Tips for Overcoming Jealousy in Relationships." Uncommon Help. Retrieved October 11, 2016. http://www.uncommonhelp.me/articles/overcoming-jealousy-in-relationships.

Van Petten, Vanessa. "5 Tips to Help Teens Deal with Jealousy." Radical Parenting, April 11, 2012. http://www.radicalparenting.com/2012/04/11/5-tips-to-help-teens-deal-with-jealousy.

Watson, Stephanie. "How to Break Up with Someone." WebMD. Retrieved October 5, 2016. http://teens.webmd.com/features/how-to-break-up-with-someone?.

Index

A

abuse, 6, 36
  exiting relationships with, 50, 52
  verbal, 39
affirmation, positive, 72, 80
aggression, 17, 19, 37, 39
anger, 10, 17, 21, 25, 36, 39, 62, 63, 71, 75, 79, 85
anxiety, 63, 64

B

betrayal, 10, 50, 79
brains, 45–46
  of adolescents, 48, 50, 98

C

cheating, 19, 37, 50
commitment, 17, 31
conflicts, 6, 58
  avoiding, 53
counselors, 72
  questions to ask, 85
critical inner voice, 13, 15, 27

criticism, 13, 19, 29, 40

D

denial, 59, 62, 69, 71
depression, 17, 21, 42, 63–64, 79, 81
disappointment, 59, 79, 94

E

emails, 19, 36, 40, 46, 47, 53, 84, 88
empathy, 17, 95
envy, 10
  as opposed to jealousy, 11
etiquette, of breakups, 53, 55–56

F

Facebook, 4, 19, 36, 47, 88
fear, 36
  of being replaced, 27
  of loss, 11, 21
flirting, 4, 17, 19, 24, 31, 37
friendships, 7, 10, 11, 13, 16, 17, 38, 39,

13, 16, 17, 38, 39, 40, 47, 50, 52, 75, 77, 79, 80, 81, 84, 86, 88, 95

G

grief, 63, 94, 96

H

hormones, 43, 48, 50, 64

I

inadequacy, feeling of, 13, 17, 27, 31
insecurity, 11, 13, 15, 17, 21, 27, 31, 36
Instagram, 4, 19, 27

K

kindness, 17, 43, 47, 53, 58, 60, 62, 77

L

lovability, 46–47
love, 7, 10, 38, 60, 72, 73, 79, 81, 95
in contrast to control, 38–39
falling in, 43, 90, 98

self, 90
loved ones, 79, 81

M

mistakes
in breakups, 31, 43, 46–47
caused by jealousy, 36

P

parents, 9, 50, 52, 75, 88
positive affirmations, 72–73
psychiatrist, 7, 17, 81–82
psychologist, 7, 13, 45–46, 72, 81–82

R

recovery, 6, 42, 71, 72, 84, 85, 98
routes, to 73, 75, 77, 79
rejection, feelings of, 45, 63
relationships, 5, 17, 25, 35–36, 45, 48, 52, 63, 69, 73, 80, 85, 90, 92, 94, 96, 98
abusive, 50, 52

anger/depression in, 21

boundaries in, 5–6, 42

damaging, 38

ending, 4, 39, 40, 45, 46–47, 50, 53, 55, 56, 60, 62, 63, 98

goal of, 33, 35

healthy, 40, 88

jealousy in, 7, 11, 19, 31, 37, 41, 42

LGBTQ, 16

limbo, 56

maintenance of, 50

open, 9, 11, 50, 59

problems in, 39–40, 47, 62, 82

value of, 46

S

sadness, 10, 17, 66, 73, 75, 77

safety, 41, 52, 55–56, 58, 77, 80

school, 4, 24, 31, 33, 47, 59, 62, 80

self-confidence, 11, 13, 15, 27, 52, 63, 67, 98

self-doubt, 13, 27, 63, 69

self-esteem, 17, 31, 37, 63, 69, 71, 77, 98

self-respect, 11, 63

socializing, 19, 21

social media, 19, 36, 37, 40, 52, 53, 80, 84

social world, 11, 46

stress, 21, 50, 64, 94

sympathy, 58, 80–81

T

texts, 4, 19, 24, 33, 36, 40, 46, 47, 52, 53, 55, 84

therapist, 35–36, 72, 81–82

V

values, 13

violence, 17, 39

W

writing, 27, 29, 35–36, 79

affirmations, 72

a blog, 80

About the Author

Tamra B. Orr is the author of numerous nonfiction books for readers of all ages. She graduated from Ball State University with a degree in education and English and has spent her life learning about the world. She and her family live in the Pacific Northwest, where she researches and writes during her working hours and goes camping and writes letters in her free time. Although she has been happily married for thirty-four years, she remembers the pain of jealousy and breaking up and has witnessed her children going through these challenges. It has taught her to value relationships and remember that everything in life contains a lesson.

Photo Credits

Cover Petrenko Andriy/Shutterstock.com; p. 5 apomares/E+/Getty Images; pp. 8–9 Hill Street Studios/Blend Images/Getty Images; p. 12 Mixmike/E+/Getty Images; pp. 14–15 JGI/Jamie Grill/Blend Images/Getty Images; p. 18 Seb Oliver/Image Source/Getty Images; pp. 20, 68–69 Image Source/Getty Images; p. 23 borchee/E+/Getty Images; p. 26 © iStockphoto.com/ValaGrenier; pp. 28–29 Image Source/Photodisc/Getty Images; pp. 30–31 -Mosquito-/E+/Getty Images; pp. 32–33 jtyler/E+/Getty Images; pp. 34–35 Sandra Hoever/Corbis/Getty Images; pp. 44–45 Tomas Rodriguez/Corbis/Getty Images; pp. 48–49 PhotoAlto/Alamy Stock Photo; p. 51 101dalmatians/E+/Getty Images; pp. 54–55 pixelfit/E+/Getty Images; p. 57 SW Productions/Stockbyte/Getty Images; pp. 60–61 Robert Crum/Shutterstock.com; pp. 64–65 VMJones/E+/Getty Images; pp. 70–71 Todor Tsvetkov/E+/Getty Images; pp. 74–75 Krakozawr/E+/Getty Images; pp. 76–77 sturti/E+/Getty Images; pp. 78–79 bowdenimages/iStock/Thinkstock; pp. 82–83, 90–91, 92–93 Hero Images/Getty Images; p. 87 martin-dm/E+/Getty Images; p. 89 Hero Images/DigitalVision/Getty Images; pp. 96–97 Jupiterimages/Pixland/Thinkstock; cover and interior pages background © iStockphoto.com/Sergei Dubrovski.

Designer: Nicole Russo-Duca; Editor and Photo Researcher: Philip Wolny